NO REASON

The Poiema Poetry Series

Poems are windows into worlds; windows into beauty, goodness, and truth; windows into understandings that won't twist themselves into tidy dogmatic statements; windows into experiences. We can do more than merely peer into such windows; with a little effort we can fling open the casements, and leap over the sills into the heart of these worlds. We are also led into familiar places of hurt, confusion, and disappointment, but we arrive in the poet's company. Poetry is a partnership between poet and reader, seeking together to gain something of value—to get at something important.

Ephesians 2:10 says, "We are God's workmanship..." *poiema* in Greek—the thing that has been made, the masterpiece, the poem. The Poiema Poetry Series presents the work of gifted poets who take Christian faith seriously, and demonstrate in whose image we have been made through their creativity and craftsmanship.

These poets are recent participants in the ancient tradition of David, Asaph, Isaiah, and John the Revelator. The thread can be followed through the centuries—through the diverse poetic visions of Dante, Bernard of Clairvaux, Donne, Herbert, Milton, Hopkins, Eliot, R. S. Thomas, and Denise Levertov—down to the poet whose work is in your hand. With the selection of this volume you are entering this enduring tradition, and as a reader contributing to it.

—D.S. Martin
Series Editor

No Reason

JACK STEWART

CASCADE *Books* · Eugene, Oregon

NO REASON

The Poiema Poetry Series

Cascade Books
An Imprint of Wipf and Stock Publishers
199 W. 8th Ave., Suite 3
Eugene, OR 97401

www.wipfandstock.com

PAPERBACK ISBN: 978-1-7252-6780-0
HARDCOVER ISBN: 978-1-7252-6779-4
EBOOK ISBN: 978-1-7252-6781-7

Cataloguing-in-Publication data:

Names: Last, First. | other names in same manner
Title: Book title : book subtitle / Author Name.
Description: Eugene, OR: Cascade Books, 2020 | Series: if applicable | Includes bibliographical references and index.
Identifiers: ISBN 978-1-7252-6780-0 (paperback) | ISBN 978-1-7252-6779-4 (hardcover) | ISBN 978-1-7252-6781-7 (ebook)
Subjects: LCSH: subject | subject | subject | subject
Classification: CALL NUMBER 2020 (print) | CALL NUMBER (ebook)

Manufactured in the U.S.A.   AUGUST 19, 2020

for Sherri

What saint strained so much,
Rose on such lopped limbs to a new life?
—THEODORE ROETHKE

. . . serious doubt is confirmation of faith.
—PAUL TILLICH

Table of Contents

Table of Contents

No Reason

Islands of algae just off the bank,
A dead fish wedged in broken cattails,
The shore grass slick and janky
In the rotten air—what
God would sacrifice himself for that?

It was hard to keep footing on the wet grass.
My heels dug lesions with every step. I had
Come with no purpose but to clear my head,
Let the measured hours lose focus.
In the dusk, had the water gone down less

Than the mud had risen? I think what I wanted
Was to want to go back. Holy narratives
Return to water. No birds. No overcast heron
Balancing on its secret, only silence sainting
The sky. Faith is a slick stone to stand upon.

I sat down and let the wet seep through my pants,
Felt the slime on my skin, listened to the pond barely
Shrug its shoulders. I felt the wind wince
A few times. Until I saw pity in the evidence,
That stagnant light, that sky stripped bare.

Part 1

A Driving Rain

The wind drives the rain sideways, and the ducks
Have sunk so far into their shoulders, they look like feathered turtles.
The orchid tree outside our porch is having a seizure.
Even the pond is trying to get away,
The ripples racing along the bank
And not looking back—

Like the cold rain driving Adam
And Eve out of Paradise,
The wet wind that soaked them cold
To the bone and denied any cover,
And their knowledge that when it stopped
All they had tended would straighten
And the green deepen and shine.

They would outrun the rain
Into the desert,
To the earth baked hard, a sterile earth
He would have to break into the barest life
To survive.
They would remember
The sun in the cedars,
The poplars aflame,
The cherry trees thick with blossoms,
The lions' manes burning along the underbrush.

Gradually the wind slows, and the rain
Bends to the softness of a willow.
Another hour and the ducks
Are coasting the bank.
Everything breathes deeply
In the returning warmth.
The prayer in the bones has ended.
The pond is as calm as black marble,
The grass silver with light.

Second Fruit

Were the other apples disappointed at not being chosen
And therefore remade themselves into
Different knowledges, so that if Adam
Had bitten into a second apple he would have
Known French, or Eve tasting another could
Have been filled with the strategies of Charlemagne
Or how to make a hoop skirt
Or the chemistry and physics of a combustion engine?

But after they admired their bodies,
Staring at each other as if
They had all the time in the world
Because that was suddenly what they wanted
More than anything else, they were
Driven out without a chance
To learn something useful.

That night, when they roasted a rabbit
Over their first fire, half a mile from
The garden that now had a locked gate,
They looked back at the small gleam
The angel's sword made in the air.
And Adam held the stick aflame
With the rabbit's thigh and waved it
Slowly in that direction. Not out of cynicism
Or bitterness, but out of longing to do what
They had done so many times before,
The mute acknowledgement of love,
And the angel then slowly, slowly, waved his sword,
Not out of sarcasm or a threat, but from his
Own solemn sadness, in his own ancient
Knowledge that sometimes forgiveness is
All that is needed, and so simple,
And yet impossible to give.

Adam's First Farm

Maybe the snow will soften the ice
That barbs the wire of the fence.
The cold keeps out more than
Angels, keeps in more than the sparse
Animals that usually graze
Along the yellow distance.
The wind won't blow his footprints
Back open. Maybe in a few days
The sky will unfold itself,
But right now his breath expands
The emptiness.

Between now and the horizon
He can figure out if anything
Is missing, and if it is, how
To name it. Winter's not yet
Familiar. He doesn't know
What it means to trespass or
Escape, only that beautiful bits of snow
Are caught like tufts of wool upon the wire.

Uncountable Winter Blossoms

First, the mud begins to soften
Where the crust of snow has melted,
And the dead leaves, crisp under the cold,

Begin to flex as they decompose.
Snow shattered over these branches for months,
But now there are only dark stains where it was.

Eve sometimes sees
Pulses of water beneath the iced-over streams
And thinks of the kicks now more frequent in her belly.

In a few months, long before their child
Can even crawl, these trees will fill
With so many blossoms the sun can't get through,

A petal for every future generation,
Or the words no one has ever said,
To teach the children she cannot imagine.

When the Pounding on the Roof Stopped

When the pounding on the roof stopped
Noah went to the doorway. The water
Dripped silver from the eaves,
And he tried not to question God.

Soon, a muddy hillside began to appear,
Some rocks soaked black. He imagined
All the work to be done, the burden
Of making no mistakes, the chance
To make amends for what he felt
Was partly his fault. He would build
The houses high on the slopes,
Breed animals that sensed
He was not to be trusted.
He would teach his grandchildren, their
Children, all the generations, obedience
And the ways of righteousness.

He made himself remember:
The treetops swaying heavy
With monkeys like the last autumn leaves,
The horns of the goats
Slipping below the surface,
And the giraffes short-necked.
Alone, he prayed for understanding
And never received an answer
That was reasonable and clear.

Samson

In an empty field at dusk,
When the weeds are swaying like veils,
Call, "Delight! Delight!"
And she will come to you from the trees.
You will feel the hot tears again
And the fingers on your loins.

When you lie down
You will hear the soft scuttling
Somewhere through the weeds
Of mice destroying a bee hive.
You can hear her undressing
Next to you.

She drapes a veil on your chest,
And the breeze moves across
The bitten dates of your eyes.
You think there are stars
Inside your head . . . .

When you feel her breasts
Pressing you down
You realize the house still stands
In the city, even you are not dead,
Nor a king,
And the tears and fingers
Are your own.

Job's Reverie

who hath given understanding to the heart?

Job 38:36

The fennel is in bloom.

He can remember when the sun
Was soft as bread, the future
A pail of clear water.

Now sores run pus between
His shoulder blades where he
Cannot reach;
Fleas burrow in his groin;
The leather of his sandals is slick
From broken blisters.

He knows the words he could throw
At God, the black scabs of syllables
Cracking into pieces
That would fall back on his head.

Will God ever turn back?
Pity seems slower than the blood
That oozed into his beard
When he dug at the boils
Enflaming his cheeks.

It would take so little
To comfort. Even less than
The sins in the dreams he has
Never had. Just a few words

Without callouses.
A slight breeze to begin
To dry his skin. His name
Spoken with sadness.

But prayers cut like thistles.
The hawks have their own meat.

The sunset is filthy,
But the clouds are tearing
Into fine shreds.
At the edge of his vision
A lizard sits stiff beside
A windfall fig, waiting
For flies.

If the *Hindenburg* Had Left from Las Vegas

Almost natural its monochrome,
The Latin, "cumulonimbus,"
An indication of what's to come,
How certain syllables contain
Disaster, fear.
                    And yet we point with joy at these:
In Fuji green, Goodyear blue,
The black and white of Sea World,
Their ironies erased in neon.
At home beneath a threat
That's almost biblical,
A marquee message in the sky,
What desire lets us forget
That Sodom was a boom town,
With dancers, lights, and splendid coins,
When heaven rained down fire?

Anselm Kiefer's *Lot's Wife*

I am nowhere on the canvas. Not even
A white mile marker to measure the distance guilt
And grief can travel. The sky is ripped white,
As if history has been thrown away,
Its horizon mud and black ash.

After the flames burned down to embers,
God sent the rain. Memory needs cattle
And vegetation, and ash can fertilize,
A powdered mineral can feed a beast's obedience.

God did not tell the prophets everything:
That I was necessary, a righteous woman weak
Enough to not forsake the even weaker,
Who knew friendship could only be reduced to char,
A perfect black that follows begging on the wind.

God dissolved me so it would not scatter,
Stirred us together, sin mixed with sorrow
For faith to survive. He did not tell them
A woman turning her face toward home
Was looking for redemption.

Duchert's *Annunciation*

(1750s, ivory, ebony, & velvet, Cleveland Museum of Art)

In the upper left corner, a cherub
Has just pulled back the ivory curtain
To reveal the most intimate
Of biblical stories.
The angel is not
Bowing to Mary because she is holy
But because he can barely sustain
The weight of the message
That God will be born.

Draped on a pew
That looks like a lectern,
She has the hair and attitude
Of an 18th-century composer,
Eyes closed,
Right hand raised
And marking time in the air.

The floor is checked in ebony and ivory
Like a chessboard,
And the angel is moving forward
In a predetermined fashion,
While she is angled
Casually, taking up several squares
And violating the game
She seems totally unaware of.

You would not call this collage,
Not with materials only the rich
Could afford and a poor
Desert woman could not imagine.
You would not call this
Sculpture or frieze or relief
With its different media.

It shouldn't be hung on a wall
But laid flat, like a book open
To where someone was reading
And got interrupted.

Or perhaps writing
And hadn't finished.

As if this is God's diary,
The page from a day when something
So astonishing happened
It would be easy to lose the moment
Right before everything changed.

What the Others Saw

As in much of Scripture, the other witnesses
Are left out. The wise men or kings
Did not lead the camels over the desert drifts
Of snow. Shelter was loaded and unloaded by rough hands,
The inventory counted with a more useful vocabulary.
The three eventually knelt on straw, but their knees
Were protected by their heavy robes.
They told the others to keep their distance,
Find fodder in another part of the stable.
The weird star still shone overhead.

And the camelmen knew the miracle of that strange sky,
How it could guide only to an unknown place,
And no one needed wisdom to prophesy
A life of danger for a child born under it.
No one needed philosophy to foresee the loneliness
Of betrayal, with maybe some red eyes pleading silently,
Begging forgiveness from that winter star in that barren sky.

El Greco's *Holy Family and Mary Magdalene*

Only in her teens, Mary is pale and tired,
And the sky shines around the smoky clouds
That hover like a halo.
She is tired but feels proud of how well
She has adjusted to this new life,
A life of flight no less,
And absentmindedly is offering
A small peach to her boy who,
Curly-headed and no longer an infant,
Is studying how he might play with it.
Joseph holds the bowl patiently—
Pears, apples, peaches,
almost all of the cherries are gone.
Magdalene is nearly asleep, collapsed
On Mary's shoulder, relieved they have
Escaped one more time. Jesus does not care
About anything but what he could do
With the peach. Mary does not look at him
Because she knows all she needs to know
About hunger. Soon he will hold the fruit
Close to his face and then put it back in the bowl,
Then take a cherry, which he will eat carefully,
As he has been taught.
Jesus likes the way cherry stems
Bend between his fingers. He does not consider
Anything sacred just because he touches it.

Bread for the Multitude

And one, from hunger and bitterness,
Wrung the loaf as if it had absorbed
All the promises he had believed.
But between hands it re-gathered itself,
The way a cloud gathers itself from within,
And they didn't see that it stayed
About the same size. He listened.
His lips sweetened. Then he slept.
When he awoke,
The ground was dusted with crumbs
Like a snow had drifted across
To cool the afternoon, and his dreams.
It lay on the backs of his hands,
The smell mixed with the grass, and there were
No flowering trees to scatter petals
And remind him of the season,
The river was too far away to whisper.
There was only the hill rubbed bare in places
From so many bodies. A lifting
Breeze. And the miraculous summer
Snow he would tell strangers about,
A brightness to last a lifetime.

Last Weeks of the Christ

I leave behind reasons:
There are none left.
The pink blossoms my mother braided
Into her hair when she was young
Would be as good as any.

No one understands the signs:
On the hills, large rocks
Drying in the sun;
Figs sweating in a deep basket;
Dingy sheep
In bloom.

I will see in Jerusalem:
A man leaning
Out of his window
Looks like a blackened piece of twine.
Children are straggling their way
Indoors.

There is a blind woman
Sewing wineskins by the temple door.
She has no reason
To speak to anyone
But herself.

The disciples
Do not see I am dead.
In the evening light, their faces
Look like snails
I gathered from the river as a boy.

Anyone could sleep safely
In the sleeves of these hills.
The grass is worn
From the sun and spotted grazing.

I am a heat shimmer to many.
Some understand.
Others
Are afraid to believe.

I have told them
I am the son,
And there are no more reasons.

The Last Supper

Pieces of torn bread on the tablecloth.
Plates empty in front of them as if they
Have just removed the halos they will wear
In a few years. Jesus holds out his arms
Like he is scolding them for such a mess.
They look startled like they are seeing it
For the first time, it couldn't be their fault.

Leonardo claimed this is the moment
Of Christ's announcement of betrayal,
And of course it is not clear who Judas is.
But what I notice is the wine—or almost
Lack thereof. No goblets. No chalice.
The Grail no bigger than a shot glass.

Yet somehow that makes sense.
A bartender measures
As reminder of the power that he serves.
We sip liqueurs between our fingertips.
It takes so little to be satisfied.
It takes so little to linger
In camaraderie. Only a heartbeat
Of belief is necessary.
By small increments we learn to taste.

Pilate's Daughter

When no one was around I'd stand
On the seat of Father's big chair
To catch flies, the velvet firm as sand.
From there, I could see the whole square
Still empty, or maybe one
Or two pushing carts, the horizon
Just swelling with blood from the new sun,
The first yellow shadows rising

Up columns. When I heard my maid
Coming down the long hall, I'd climb down.
She smiled at my mischief and led
Me along the echoing stone
Corridors toward Father's voice
And Mother's silence, and the bland
Smells of breakfast. She told no one, kissed
Me on the head, and washed my hands.

Pittoni's *Magdalene*

As in a dance, she
Dips the cross, the image
Of Jesus barely bones,
And she herself is nearly
Bones, hair tangled and robe loose
And dingy. The angels, upper left,
Are merely heads and shoulders.
They do not sing, but she
Ignores them anyway,
Swaying slightly to the quiet
Music of her prayer—if
She hears even that. The bible
Lower left has been forgotten,
And the skull next to it
Is nothing compared to the frail
Man she now bends to.
This is not a pietà,
But serious romance,
The slow dip in the dance
An act of trust, a promise
She will raise him up
Again, until they are both
Stable, close, and ready
To move forward, face to face.

Jerome

The lion has hunted today
And sleeps in the shade of the olive tree,
His tail twitching occasionally,
His sides seeming hardly to move
Because breath . . . Breath is another food
And he is yet full. And yet,
In his sleep he licks the blood
That darkens his mouth.
What should I make of this life
You have fashioned, O Lord,
This life that bears
A heavy crown of thorns for its mouth,
And yet nuzzles my hand,
Licks my hair when I've been sleeping?

The rock of the cliffs is bland
Of color, the olive small,
And water scarce. What lives
Feeds upon light and earth
Or returns to dust. And yet still there are tufts
Growing in the crevices of rock,
Strands of dust that are stronger
Than the shock of my beard, which grows from blood.
I am truly hunted, Lord,
The sand from these walls dusting my sleep
And reminding me of the future
I possess. Even the water
That you send for me to drink,
The little pools from which I fill my gourds
When it has rained—I have
Seen my image fade from year to year.
And what is left of me when all that remains
Is a clayey spot where the water was?
The pen is brittle in my hand.

Its scratching sounds like someone
Digging for water, far away.
I look with amazement
At the letters I have written for you.
Each one, eventually,
Will fade, the paper flake
Into grains of sand. And still
I write more, restless and weary
And hunted, desirous
Of finding your name beneath my pen,
Your grace upon my lips.

The lion falls in and out of sleep.
What little wind there is
Gathers into shadows,
Frightens the pages of my book.

Dear God, I will embrace the setting of the sun
And search the darkness of your mouth,
Search this page I can no longer see but hear,
Until your words and mine are one.

Monostich

On this triptych we have three saints,
                        On this one three stories.
Sometimes they knew each other,
                        But usually not.

In what order do we view them? The paint
That was once wet changed almost immediately
To a color different from itself. It has been chipping
For seven centuries as if it, also, is
Dissatisfied with the miracle.

                        Here is a single portrait,
A monostich of a life,
But surely there was once a mother next to him,
Who sometimes rubbed his shoulders when he couldn't sleep,
Or friends who wished him safety
On his last, dusty journey.
Now they are just blank walls, the empty space
Not even framed by light.

I would rather contemplate the unrecorded dead.
Just their absence is revelation
Of a holy mystery. Just as on either side

Of this line is something so profound it can't be said.

Mary and the Ashes

I.
In the dark back of the tavern,
The smell of sweat warmed,
And the candles by the bar
Were points of light between
The moving clouds of bodies.
There would be no room later,
Not even on the benches,
But someone mumbled—
Perhaps in sarcasm,
Perhaps not—there was a stable
A few miles away where the brutal wind
Might be less brutal.
And you hoped there might
Be hay, there might
With the good fortune of forgetfulness
Be a saddle blanket
Or even a saddle that, upside down,
Could cup an infant against
The cold of the hard-packed earth.
Joseph walked in front as screen.
The snow was still an inch deep
And hard, though three days old.

II.
There was a little straw, and a feed trough
You placed between two beasts.
When the shepherds came, they
Lifted it to the edge of their fire,
Where you slept for
The first time in two days.
The next day, they were gone,
But they left the warm ashes

You and Joseph scooped into the manger,
The soft, dead ashes on which to settle your child,
Not knowing the strange
Phoenix he would become,
His arms spread wide as if
In flight, risen muscular
In an arid land, his chest
Ruddy in the spring light.

Michelangelo's Milano *Pieta*

(his last sculpture and unfinished)

1.
Framed by a hard shell of hair, Mary's face
Is a potato baked in clay, half broken free;
Christ's features, downcast, erased
By the chisel that tapped
Scrofula into stone. He has an old man's chest
But a swimmer's legs: muscular thighs,
Feet that look as if they were made
For churning water.
On the cusp of aging, this long-legged Christ
Preached devotion that curved like
A shoreline's fibula.

2.
A huge arm is emerging from the marble
As if dusted free by the sculptor-archeologist.
It hangs mid-air, big as Tiberian Law,
Attached to a rod that is jabbed
Into Jesus' ribs.
               Jagged at the shoulder,
It looks as if Michelangelo
Tore it from some Roman torso,
That marble now bright white
From hemorrhaging.

3.
               Mary's left hand is dissolving
Into her son's chest,
Past chisel-scars that look like bandages,
To his heart still warm and slick with blood.
Her right arm has almost given out.
A son should not die before his mother.

4.
He will die forever.
And she will forever hear
The chisel's slow,
Death-rattle metronome.

Pieta

(after a Vesperbild by the Master of Rabenden, 1515–1520)

Thin as an old man in Mary's arms,
His beard wispy, he looks so tired,
No one will let him sleep—he drapes
Across her lap, all elbows and knees
Like a half-opened jackknife.

What can she do but cradle
The angles of a body she no longer
Understands? She looks at his legs—
They did not break his legs.
His hands offer the large black coins
Of useless scabs. His lips are cracked.

Last night, she sat in the dark with silhouettes.
That's what words are, he taught them.

A few weeks ago, his eyes began to darken
Like bruises. Every night, someone washed the dust
From his feet. When he spoke to a stranger,
He would touch them on the hand or forearm.

She does not stroke his hair because in death
He needs to sleep, but she mouths the words
She wishes he had said.

Part 2

At Home with Angels

They used to love the limelight,
Showering upon the choreography of daily life
The fireworks spreading from their wings,
And the vast production
Of dreams. But nowadays
They're more reserved, always choosing
To stand to the side,
The way the bottle of wine
Always defers
To the bowl of fruit in the still life.
At my house, you sometimes embarrass them.
When you surprise one
Leaning against the windowsill,
Caressing the curtain.
Or humming a second longer
When the air conditioning quits.

First Lights

On days like today
When it's sunny and cold,
I think about the first time
I heard their voices.

The afternoon teased color from the grass.
The regular angels circled the Prado
And you could hear them when they flew too low,
Their bellies brushing the tops of the trees,
And the trees swaying afterwards,
Like on springs. And occasionally
A sympathetic one who had tried to watch us
Too closely would get tangled
In the branches of a large elm,
His light slashing the branches back and forth
For a full five minutes.
I could never catch his words.

And yet now, when I'm lonely
And feeling caught,
It all comes clear, the soft commands
Of the winter sun saying, *Yes,*
This patch of color's not enough,
This world is incomplete,
But have you ever dreamed
Of such exquisite emptiness,
Such striving in the dark,
The length these buds must travel up to air?
Bury your love and wait, wait.
It will find its way.
The cross, any cross,
Is a blood feather growing from the angel's heart.

Mihrab

Cleveland Museum of Art

Light flares on the ceramic,
Stretches its wings.

I want to press
My forehead against the cool tiles,

Feel the faintest ridges
Of those painted flowers.

Of all the destinies,
Who would want to be a saint,

Yet who wouldn't want to hear the words
For what can't be said,

Feel the shadow of God's heartbeat
In his own

Just once?

The Hummingbird Moth

The hummingbird moth
Comes out when night falls,
Darting around the bushes
Under the yellow, front-door light.
Not feathered, he is covered
With dusty brown hairs,
Looking more like a shriveled
Boxwood leaf than the ripened fruit
Of his namesake, and seems
Unsure what to stab, hesitant
And mostly missing, unless
It's air he jabs and eats.

I like that there are four
Or five of them, a little pack
That swerve around each other,
Unlike the vibrant, buoyant tease
That flies alone and knows
It's on display. I like how
The hummingbird moth
Does not need showy flowers,
But rather the small ones
On a bush, the ones
Unnoticed on their own.

But certainly he must
Be complex in some way,
How his wings work, for instance,
Or the accuracy of his antennae.

Complex, and worth studying.
Like kindness or listening,
Those two God created on
The eighth day, after

He rested and realized
Something was missing.
Something essential that moves
From one heart to another,
Going by the sky, the stars,
Or any light it can find.

The Annunciation

Even before she felt anything stir in her body,
It suddenly occurred to her,
He would move inside a different language,
Would use words she had never used
But perhaps had wanted to. And it wasn't
From sensing the future responsibility
Of motherhood, but she looked up, almost as if
She had remembered something she had to do
Later in the day and was relieved
She had not forgotten. No birds
Were singing, though the sky was bright,
But she did not notice. Instead, she finished
Kneading the bread, took out the knife
To scale the fish. She would take more time
With the dinner tonight, would serve it
With softer hands, with no clear reason
In her mind, no change in her heart, but simply
To celebrate Joseph's return for the evening.
She pushed her hair from her face
With the back of her hand, a fish scale
Hanging in a dark strand like a star.

Making the Lace Bands

for my wife

She leans over the sewing machine
As if studying a book big enough
To need both hands to hold
It open. The subject is so important
It requires all of her concentration.
Philosophy, perhaps—say, Niebuhr—
Or an argument of Augustine's.
But her mind is making something new,
A connection that flows out between
Her hands in one piece, a pattern
They never imagined. Six strips,
Seven strips, in an evening she
Will have something as logical
And surprising as a poem.
Unlike the others, though, she knows
Its future, can predict
What people will say. On Easter
She will slide the dress over her daughter's
Shoulders like good weather. Fasten
The beauty pins, smooth the bows. Other
Little girls will wear its echoes.
In six months she will store it
Carefully. In twenty years,
Her daughter will lift it out and stare
At the absence of dust, a slight
Crimp in the ribbons, and the bands of lace
Almost breathing in the air.

El Greco's Barmaid

In small town life, lovers are grist
For any gossip's mill, even when the barmaid
Stays at home, thinking about the cool grass
By the river, watching the moon pass
Thinner and thinner, until the heart's made
Love into a diet of Christ

And perfect shadows, perfect kisses.
Where the water is brushed out long and black
In its own mirror, and the sun
Brightens her bedclothes empty as sin,
And she ties the ragged curtains back
Only after she pins her hair and dresses.

Sisley, *Snow at Veneux*

Snow is much harder than haystacks,
Not symmetrical in the drifts
Pushed to the side of the road.
If the cold increases,
It will be tinged with blue.
In the early morning
Or early evening, as the shadows deepen,
The surface looks smudged with ashes.

Sisley painted it so honestly,
The shallow wheel ruts and footprints dabbed with mud,
The bushes capped with snow on their shoulders
As if they are waiting for a train.
The roofs of the houses have been whitewashed,
The trees are budding with white leaves.

The couple strolling toward me
Are still too far away for me to tell
If their cheeks and noses are red.
His bare hands are in his pockets,
And she wears the thin gloves of the middle class.
Her skirt is blue, and the sky is lavender.
In this late afternoon, the snow has melted enough
That the road is soft,
And he occasionally takes her by the elbow
And guides her around a puddle.
The snow fell heavily this morning,
But now the air is clear.
They do not talk much.
Her shawl is warm enough.
The ground will soon begin
To stiffen with patches of ice.
She wants to see through falling snow again,
Its lace veil,

A shower of rice coming down around her,
The warmth of an arm around her waist,
A silence that could hold anything,
A lavender sky.

The Shape of the Cold

The egrets are hunched into their necks
Like melted candles. The ducks
Have gathered on the far bank.
We can all be thankful

No snow is forecast, even though
It would be beautiful, slowly
Rippling the pond like what
Fish rise to, the subtlest

Light imaginable. Wouldn't
You like to walk here a moment
Before the birds unruffle themselves
And contemplate flight, contemplate

A sky nearly as white
As they are? How, as they rise, they might
Be absorbed as completely as
Elijah surely was?

It would be as close to miracle
As we could ever get, that mirrored
Absence above, when suddenly
The living are simply

Gone. No one would call it an act of God,
But that does not mean it is not
Worth wonder, that it is not beyond
Explaining, standing by a pond

In the early morning without words,
A man and woman with faces toward
The sky, with nothing to hold
In their hands but the shape of the cold.

The Elect

All over this snow-laden town
Thousands of Popes have been elected,
The white smoke rising from what seem
To be every chimney. Gray as stones,

Even the people breathe the white smoke
Of approval as they shovel
Walks or jog the wrecked roads. Under
The glittering white miters of

The pines, someone holy has been
Agreed upon, someone who knows
How fierce the heart is when
It scrounges. How, without choice,

The winter sun itself scrounges.
Dead leaves search for shadows. Birds shrug
Into their wings. Maybe the Pope
Himself will pull on boots and dig,

Jabbing all the way to the brick,
His blessed scarf hanging to his knees.
Then sow the salt to melt what's left,
Ignoring that another freeze

Will descend every night for months.
He will look at the nothingness
He has created and judge it good enough
For now. Which is his lesson

Every mass until Easter:
That the good life is spent getting rid
Of things that come back. The moon
Is thin like the collar of a priest.

When the Air Is Cold Enough

I love how the morning crust
Breaks when you head across a field,

But here I can stand without
Having to blow into my hands or clap
To keep them warm
Or stamp my feet.

I enjoy remembering snow—
Wrapping the azaleas in burlap against a freeze,
Carefully pushing Christmas lights into holly.

I love the way snow improvises,
The way it falls relaxed
But with purpose.

The way snow and moonlight conspire
To light up the back yard
Like good news,
Like an x-ray that shows everything
With nothing amiss.

So easily ruined,
Marred by mud or soot,
It is pushed to the side,
Gray as a cold-fogged windshield.

And yet the drift against the telephone pole
Is still white five feet above the curb.

I love how when the air is cold enough
The snow does not dissolve into itself.
A parable for love's slow gathering.

Lungs

Fog on the x-ray,
Two breaths on a cold windowpane at night—

My chest swells and falls
As the doctor says it should.
I imagine two white hyacinths
Turning ever so slightly in the breeze.

I don't have to do anything
To make them bloom.
I don't have to cover them against the cold.

They take care of themselves,
Close to each other,
Two bouquets in my body.

The doctor gives them to the nurse.

I give them to you,
As I have for 22 years.

They sing a song you listen to
When I sleep—
Of flowers blooming in darkness,
Of warm breath you can see,

Of moonlight in two lungs,
Like lanterns I bear.

These two lanterns glowing with moonlight
On a screen.

Misconception

The snow heals,
Scabbing the earth and the tips
Of trees, fastening bark
To itself, and weighting the stones
To teach them the weight
Of moss. It burns the cheeks
Of the man walking next door,
To remind him
Of what he loves.
What more could God do
Than to provide white,
Which is the most important
Color to the painter
So he can begin, and the writer,
And the medieval monk
Knew he depended on white
To set the birds in *O*s, train the vines
Up *T*s, and wind the serpent
Along the *F*'s highest branch
Of the Latin that made
The sacred Greek known.

I grew up hating snow
But learned
What it means to be overcome,
And to overcome,
And how to take in hand
My father's death.
Cardinals pulsed in the holly;
A white-tail deer erased itself
In its leaving.
What more could evil fear
Than when a man and woman
Concentrate on nothing more

Than the need for sanctuary?
The holy place, a philosopher said,
Is where "the infinitely removed

Makes itself near and present,
Without losing its remoteness."
The trees shine with emptiness.
Animals burrow into the brittle husk.
Broken bones are stronger when they heal,
And the breaking begins
When the snow begins to fall.

Part 3

For My Stillborn Bothers

In the dusk of this morning
The street still wet from last night's shower,
A few birds tentative.
A few pine cones lie in water
Under the tree across the street.
In the puddle of branches,
Silhouettes are soft and graceful.
Each breath demands so much be done,
Even in the quiet of this morning.
How can I bless the shadows
That have stretched out their hands to me?
They have told me, *Go on, brother, go on.*
What is light, brother, is yours.

Virtuoso of Silence

for Samuel Sidney Stewart

I remember the stories of his music
But not the music,
Remember the vibraphone
Like a radiator
Against the wall in the basement,
But not the mallets' staccato
Or the blur of his wrists.
I lifted 78s, black dinner plates
Of Dvorak or Benny Goodman,
Felt the heft of such music,
But had no phonograph
To play them on, broken as it was
In the corner, like a car's grill.

My grandmother sent me one
Of his saxophones,
A C-melody, no longer made,
Probably the one he played at boarding school,
The reeds, sixty years old, frayed,
The wooden mouthpiece cut-grooved
From his teeth.

I remember my mother
Getting the phone call and turning to me,
Saying, "He's dead,"
Not telling me
He was found at the kitchen table,
Slumped over the pool cue of his rifle.

My grandmother never closed
The lid of the piano
Or tucked away the sheet music,
All the notes like tadpoles
That will grow no further.

I cannot mourn the loss
Of what I never heard,
But never needed lessons
To play that silence,

What I can't turn off or put away,
That oldest song
You can't get out of your head,
And the words you'll never forget.

Stethoscopic

So convinced of the existence
Of a rattle, my father made
My brother kneel in the back seat
Of the Buick and move the stethoscope
Across the window, the top of the seat,
The ledge below the glass,
As they drove around the neighborhood.
Nothing came through that long black tube
But my brother's fear of being seen.

Alone, stiff in the vinyl chair
At the bedside, my mother knew
The moment of my father's death
Without a stethoscope. Nor did
She ring for a nurse, but sat frozen
While the heating vent at the window
Blew the curtains slightly.
Then she bowed.

I found his old one coiled in a cabinet.
I put it on as a curiosity,
Listened to my heartbeat, then laid it back.
I don't know what I'd expected to hear
Inside the slide of my family's breathing,
Or what to imagine that doesn't make a sound.
Where would I place that cold knob
To listen for devotion?
What would I set my ear upon
To catch the regular rhythm of hope?

Saint Hieronymus and the Brown Egg

You can't write and peel a boiled egg
At the same time. The bits of shell
Look like flakes from a fresco, maybe the elbow
Of a saint. What would he have said
About food and about speech, putting
Together a meal of syllables,
Which is what prayer was to him, to fill
His mouth and the belly of his lungs? But
Maybe he also boiled an egg, in rainwater,
Two chickens pecking in the dust
While he fed the small flame
With a fist of mold-spotted leaves.

The last curve of shell lifts free.
If the saint had lived on a coast,
He could have sprinkled a little seawater
On it, a faint dust of salt when it dried.
He would have said God
Allows an egg. The firm white
Resists the knife or teeth at first, just as
The soul resists the blade of the Word.

The white has little taste.
I use my knuckle on another,
The force crazes the shell,
The lines spread out the width
Of the saint's plaster eye.
What do you bless most,
The hunger or the food?
Flakes of shell on a plate,
A vision in pieces.
A blessing whispered
Like words being erased.

Buccellati Hedgehog

Plinth by plinth,
These masterpieces of craftsmanship:

    A swan-necked centerpiece;

    Chess set with ivory tents
        For the Saracens of Saladin
        Facing the onyx rooks of Richard.

    The filigree of this tiara for a Romanian princess
        Is more delicate than a rain-shimmering spider web.

Yet
The hand of God is most obvious
In this silver hedgehog about the size of a flat hairbrush.

St. Francis said to find
And admire
The overlooked,
Those that shone only with sweat
And their apologies.

As dawn began to swell, they
Broke the earth with old picks,
Scraped the ground with blunt hoes.
They found their way home by the candles
Of goldenrod.

When did the sparrows start singing under the eaves?

What We Feed On

A few brown leaves on the walk gust
Into the bushes. Curly-tailed lizards,
Their shadows rolled up on their backs.
They've learned they are harder to kill
If they cast no shadow.

They do not print the dust
When they move, either. Their tracks
Are green response. Still, they neither
Disappear in heavy mist
Nor barter color with the sun,

Just a monk's rough dull brown
That blends with burned grass or the long dead.
They eat their own. Just like the crescent
Moon feeds on itself. Or eyes on darkness.
Or time on the belly of Christ

When he hung on the cross, time feeding
On itself unending. Now the head
Of a shriveled berry appears.
Fallen, though the bush never shook.
Like a minute from the years.

Maximilian's Hawk

Hunting is all it imagines,
Horizoned only by time.
The hood, bejeweled as
Elaborately as a diadem: emeralds,
Rubies, two onyx studs over
Eyes that can tell the difference
Between a breeze in the grass
And something to be killed.
Maximillian did not commission
It for his vanity,
But to honor one skilled
In God's oldest determination:
What should live and what should die.
The thongs hanging from its feet
Will become bloody rosaries.

Turner's *Burning of the House of Lords and Commons, 1834*

The flames rise like the plume on a cavalier's hat.
The fire barge will never get there in time
Coasting so slowly, looking more like a pier
Than a vessel that could help. For their effort,
The brigade does have a better view than the people
On the shore, jagged smudges of men and women bereft
Of everything but wonder. Just the scale
Of the disaster oranges the water.
The harbor is too deep to actually boil,
But no one would think to dip a foot in.
                                    A boy
Lingers away from the crowd, just off the canvas,
Enough on his own to contemplate whether this fact
Confirms or denies the existence of God. Fire blacks
Out the stars, blinds those who stare at it too long.
Does someone have to die for him to question or affirm?
Eventually the wind will blow the smoke back into
Clean air. Eventually the ashes will be carted away,
Gratitude for what survived become fatigue
With what was lost. Like most of them, he lost nothing,
But he still wants to understand what it did to him.
Why, even when the beach is covered with snow, will he
Think of how warm the pebbles were, how he wanted
To put some in his pockets, or even hold
Against his cheek? The harbor pants
Under the cool sky. Flocks of gulls
Break into pieces in the early light.

Looking from the Garden Wall of the Pitti Palace Down into Florence

On fine evenings, Catherine de Medici watched
The Duomo smolder in the basin of the town,
The bells silent, people hurrying in different
Directions like beads from a broken rosary. If
She looked away, did she notice the sky
Was unremarkable, maybe thatched with clouds?
She loved the moon faces of Bronzino's portraits
In the long hallways lit by candles,
Their pure broad foreheads and troubled eyes,
But here she could stop thinking, not even breathe,
As the dark stiffened like brocade.

She did not care for mornings,
The chipped roof tiles bright in the sun,
The beads re-strung at the church door
And slipping through fingers of markets and alleys.
Three weeks after she was born, both her parents
Were dead. Down in the piazza below,
The women sweeping ashes that lifted into pigeons
Would live forever.

The Seder

According to the story,
The Jews marked their doors with lamb's-blood
To keep the Angel of Death away.
And how many Egyptians he took that night
Is impossible to say; their breath
Suddenly gone, they stared
Wide-eyed at their parents in disbelief,
Not understanding, accusing.
Tonight we eat haroses and matzah,
And you pour the wine for Elijah
And set it in the middle of the table.
We pray to remember, we pray
For what we never knew, the night
Of children dying all around us
And the wail of mothers who couldn't understand.
We don't have any candles,
But the wine flickers like melted wax,
Shining even in its depths.
The zucchini, the mushrooms, are crisp
And greasy like the burned lips of the dead,
The onions stripped from the sockets of the earth.
We eat, just like our prayer, all
That we've read about, what we've turned
Into a way to forgive.

We relax when the ceremony's over
And the dishes are cleared away.
I make a silly toast to all of us,
And Amy asks if Elijah
Has taken a sip yet.
The door is open to let the warm spring air in,
The smell of the magnolias.
The potted ferns dangle
Like huge spiders over the porch.

We laugh, and I want to dance,
I want to prove that we're all alive,
I want to sweat until I can't remember
Anything but the dark girl who pleased Pharaoh
In the picture books, the dark childless girl
Trying to save her neighbors' children.
I want to dance with her and make her believe
That it's all over, that the children
Are only dreaming in Gaza, in Kosovo,
In Armenia, in Mosul,
In all the places that we cannot touch.
I want to hold her in my arms
Until we both believe her love
Was a success and everyone is free
And drinking with Elijah in the streets,
Everyone singing and dancing.

But how do you convince the past?
How do you love a woman who's been dead three thousand years?
I want to tell her a story that will make her smile,
Tell her that Pharaoh's changed his mind,
That there are no more Pharaohs in the world.

When you pour Elijah's wine down the drain
I want to know whose blood marks this house,
And what angels pass over us nightly,
Their shadows blackening the magnolias,
Their feathers stained with pollen, their smell
Making the neighborhood dogs go wild.

Grace after the Service

When you press your palms together,
You can turn away from
Yourself. The tabebuia bells lay shattered
Across the lawn, their yellow still bright in the moonlight,
The air heavy, breathing,
Grieving for itself,
The mountain to the east hooded like a hawk.
As a child, I stared at the angels perched
Glowing in the tops of the magnolias.
I watched starlings rise, whirling like shreds
Of a mourning veil.

When you press your palms together, you can turn away from yourself
And everything else.
I felt the wind on my ankles,
Like something that had come through high grass,
Even though the church had a well-trimmed lawn.
The singing had swelled like a bruise.
The sermon bruised. The Scripture
Gave me doubts. I looked at the twisted branches of the tabebuias,
Enough flowers left to show something grows from deformity.
I understood. You look up at the moon, you look up at the sun,
Or the rain. It doesn't matter. You lift your face
When you can't go on.

A Flat of Begonias

They have no scent and look like cabbages
Gone bad in the produce bin of the supermarket,
The blossoms like shriveled radishes
Dumped on top, a salad a stock boy makes

After hours. They say Jesus' wounds
Dried to the color of a begonia leaf.
Until finally, darker than coffee grounds,
They flaked away. All that was left

Was a bright pink scar in the center.
But neither begonias, nor you, nor I, can explain
What happened after. Or why I spend
The day dirtying my hands to get them clean.

Shroud of Turin

If it is his,
It is not
The shadows of cheekbones
Or hollows of eyes,
The knuckles of hands that blessed,
But blotches from the fig-stained spit
Of the soldiers who passed
His dumped body.

They left him in the smell
Of dust and olive,
His followers standing
Out of the way.

If it weren't for this sealed glass,
The cotton would rot.
The trees were everywhere,
The fruit a staple to survive.

I buy fig jam for my children.
I send Christmas baskets
With dried figs and apricots.
I would never deny
History.
I just believe that sweetness,
Even shriveled by dry air and sun,
Can outlast contempt.

Balancing the Flame

St. Stephanskirche, Vienna

Gothic grappling hook to heaven,
When it was rebuilt in the 14th century
The limestone must have shone brighter
Than the December snow.
Now soot-shadows climb the walls
And can't be scrubbed away.

Inside, the light is also dim,
Even over the altar's marble ember.
I drop a Euro in the cup.
In the musty oxygen,
The candle releases
A thread of smoke.

Most prayers begin in failure.
Like a match in an unsteady hand,
My *amen* always falters.
In what trembling air,
On what wick of words
Can I balance its flame?

The Ruined Saint

The slashed body
Hanging from a branch,
A harness of blood
Streaming over the shoulders . . . .

From a gash on one leg
A gemmed rosary of a rivulet
Slides down his calf and over his foot
To drip between his toes.

The miracle is that it stops mid-air
And swings lightly in the breeze.
Then the sun takes it
And begins to sew his wounds closed,
The sutures of blood cleansing his body
Until he hangs a shining death for
The ignorant to believe.

This isn't
Just a story. This isn't just
A reliquary for bones that no one found.
If in the beginning was the Word, you make
Your prayer beads out of syllables,
Out of prayers themselves.

They shaved his head.
They had long knives
And rope, a sharpened walking staff,
A hoe,
And whatever else
Their hate could find.

The saint is dead,
And I can only speak in martyred words,
I can only speak to bless.

The Vita Nuova

From the early morning grass, gnats rise, a small blur
Hovering. Above the broken heart-
Shaped leaves fallen from the ashes, a part
Of last night's storm, they filter the air
With constant movement. The red mouth
Of God, burning like the torn yellow
Ends of broken branches, draws into air new marrow,
The dusted body of a moth.
     These have been my dreams every
Morning over coffee, and through them
I see the beads broken on the stem,
The Host risen in its fury
To prepare the world, and Its shadow
Cool over the lawn: the life I will know.

Acknowledgements

The following poems have appeared in some form in or are forthcoming in the following journals:

Poetry: "At Home with Angels," "El Greco's Barmaid"

American Literary Review: "The Seder"

The Journal of the American Medical Association: "Stethoscopic"

Image: "The Last Supper," "Bread for the Multitude," "The Ruined Saint," "Monostich"

Poetry Salzburg Review: "Pittoni's *Magdalene*," "When the Pounding on the Roof Stopped" (earlier titled "When the Flood Came")

Nimrod: "Making the Lace Bands"

The Zeppelin Reader: "If the *Hindenburg* Had Left from Las Vegas"

The Old Red Kimono: "The Vita Nuova"

White Pelican Review: "The Annunciation"

Poem: "Lungs," "For My Stillborn Brothers"

Ponder Review: "Adam's First Farm"

Relief: "Second Fruit," "Pilate's Daughter," "The Elect," "The Shape of the Cold"

California Quarterly: "Samson"

New Ulster: "Sisley, *Snow at Veneux*," "Looking from the Garden Wall of the Pitti Palace Down into Florence"

The Black Warrior Review: "Jerome"

Drastic Measures: "A Flat of Begonias"

Connecticut River Review: "Turner's *The Burning of the House of Lords and Commons, 1834*"

Rabbit: "Virtuoso of Silence"

Blue Mountain Review: "Saint Hieronymus and the Brown Egg"

The Perch: "Grace After the Service"

The Galway Review: "No Reason"

"First Lights" won the Academy of American Poets Prize, Emory University

"Misconception" won the Alabama Teachers' Literary Award

The Poiema Poetry Series

www.ingramcontent.com/pod-product-compliance
Lightning Source LLC
LaVergne TN
LVHW041203080426
835511LV00006B/717